A Devotional Throughout the day

Kevin Bandoli

WESTBOW
PRESS®
A DIVISION OF THOMAS NELSON
& ZONDERVAN

Copyright © 2024 Kevin Bandoli.

All rights reserved. No part of this book may be used or reproduced by any means, graphic, electronic, or mechanical, including photocopying, recording, taping or by any information storage retrieval system without the written permission of the author except in the case of brief quotations embodied in critical articles and reviews.

WestBow Press books may be ordered through booksellers or by contacting:

WestBow Press
A Division of Thomas Nelson & Zondervan
1663 Liberty Drive
Bloomington, IN 47403
www.westbowpress.com
844-714-3454

Because of the dynamic nature of the Internet, any web addresses or links contained in this book may have changed since publication and may no longer be valid. The views expressed in this work are solely those of the author and do not necessarily reflect the views of the publisher, and the publisher hereby disclaims any responsibility for them.

Any people depicted in stock imagery provided by Getty Images are models, and such images are being used for illustrative purposes only. Certain stock imagery © Getty Images.

Scripture quotations marked KJV are taken from the King James Version.

ISBN: 979-8-3850-3513-7 (sc)
ISBN: 979-8-3850-3514-4 (e)

Library of Congress Control Number: 2024920886

Print information available on the last page.

WestBow Press rev. date: 10/31/2024

Love the Lord thy God

When we love the Lord thy God. We should have fullness of joy in our heart. We need to remember what he did on the cross. For us and all of mankind. We can show God's love by loving our neighbor. When we sing praises to our God. We should be willing to share our faith with others. I thank you dear Lord. For that free gift of eternal life. Once we accept Jesus as our Lord and Savior. We have that new life, that new relationship with the Lord Jesus.

Prayer

> Dear Lord I love you with my whole being. I pray for the loss with all my whole heart. Lord, I thank you for dying for me on that old rugged cross.

The faith of a Mustard Seed

Matthew 22:36-40, Hebrews 11:1-2

Gracious Lord, thank you for your word. In the 119 Psalm and in verse 97 comes to mind. As we meditate on God's word. That increases our faith in you precious Lord.The parable of the mustard seed comes to mind. In Matthew 13: 31-32 this parable comes to mind. The parable of the mustard seed is a great example of the power of our Lord. When we exercise our faith the Lord comes through for us. Also this parable teaches us that we need trust in our precious Lord and Savior. In the parable a man sowed a seed in the field. Which indeed is the least of all the seeds. Among the herbs it becometh a tree. So that the birds of the air come and lodge in the branches thereof.

Prayer

Father I ask that thou increase my faith.

The Faith of the Centurion

Matthew 8:5-13, Hebrews 11:1

The faith of the centurion as a great truth of the Lord's word. I always think of this account. I Look at his strong faith in the Lord Jesus. He was not ashamed of Jesus Christ; the lamb without blemish. When he told Jesus that he was not worthy to be under the same roof. Jesus said there was not such great faith in all of Israel. The main point is the centurion was a gentile. Because most jews at this time did not believe that Jesus was the Messiah. That they had been waiting for. In Hebrews 11:3 the Holy Bible tells us that the Word of God is what strengthens our faith. We can have that faith that the centurion had.

Prayer

Lord help my faith grow. Let me be that child you want me to be.

The Passion of the Christ

Isaiah 53:1-12

What is that passion that the Lord is trying to show us in Isaiah 53:6. The verse goes like this. All we like sheep have gone astray; we have turned every one to his own way; and the Lord has laid on him the iniquity of us all. When I think about this passage, It shows us how much God the Father loves us. My greatest day of my life was when I accepted Jesus as my Lord and Savior. Titus 3:4-6 tells us that we need to be saved. I was eight years old.I was at an easter egg hunt at a Baptist church in Eau Claire WI. The Pastor asked me if I knew who Jesus was. I told him I was not sure. He asked me if I wanted to accept Jesus into my heart. I told him that I did. In the spring of 1969. I became a child of Jesus Christ.

Prayer

Lord Jesus I pray for the ones that read this devotional. That they have that salvation experience. In Jesus' mighty name.

The Great Comforter

The key verse John 14:26
John 14:16-31

The Lord Jesus promises us the great comforter the Holy Ghost. Who dwells within our spirit. Once we expected Jesus as our Lord and Savior. He is our teacher, comforter and counselor. When we feel down and depressed. He gives us peace and joy. That Jesus speaks of in John 14:27. Also in John 16:33. He tells us to be of good cheer. He has overcome the world. We can have the blessed assurance that he dwells in our heart. Remember God loves you. He wants his grace to flow through your heart. Please be not afraid to share about Jesus and the receiving of the Holy Ghost.

Prayer

Father I pray that I may receive your son Jesus the great Lord and Savior.

Ask Seek and Knock

Matthew 7:7-11 key verse Matthew 7:7

When we go to the Lord we must be in his will. How do we know that? We pray and read his words. That is how we find his will for our lives. When we go to seek him. We need to repent of our sin. So we have a clear picture of what his will is. When we knock on his door. He will open the door so we can enter. But he will not push himself on us. Because he wants that relationship with us. We need to remember that he loves us. Ask seek knock all three important in our relationship with him.

Prayer

Lord help me to ask, seek and Knock on his door. He will enter into our lives in a way. That we will know that it is him.

The Parable of the Sower

Matthew 13: 3-23
Key verse Psalms 119: 105

Jesus is telling this parable. He is trying to show how important it is that we read his words. We need to give him our whole heart. In Psalms 119 : 97 the verse tells us that we are to meditate on his word; all day. So that we live the life that brings him glory, honor and praise. We know that he is a holy God and we should always give him reverence also. We should always always want to share our faith with others. The Bible tells us in Psalms 119: 105 the word is a lamp unto, our feet and a light for our path.

Prayer

Lord help me to understand your word. So it multiplies
a hundred fold.

The Parable of the Weeds

Matthew 13: 24-30
Key verse: Hebrews 12:2

It's our responsibility to focus on Jesus. The author and finisher of our faith. When we are the wheat we are following Jesus. He is responsible for separating the wheat from the tares. When we have the life that Jesus wants us to live. We can be that true witness that Jesus wants us to be. The Father sent his Son to die for our sins. When we are that witness Jesus wants us to be. The Lord can do miracles in the lives of others. He can also do miracles in our lives. When people come to Jesus. The glory of God has been reached. That should be our goal as followers of Jesus.

Prayer

Father help me to be that true witness for you dear Lord.

Abstain From Evil

1 Thessalonians 5:15-23

The Lord wants us to have a spirit of goodness. Not a spirit of evil. When we take time to spend time in the Bible. We are getting a stronger relationship with the Lord. When we spend time in prayer. We make our heart and soul right with the Lord. Then we are able to direct our sinful nature in the right direction. The Father and the Son are pleased with the direction we are heading. The Holy Ghost is the one who directs us. When we cling to evil that pushes us from the Lord for a season. Our witness is severely damaged. Others will not see the Lord in us. We will not be able to share the Gospel with others. When we walk in humility we will be an asset for the kingdom of heaven.

Prayer

Father help me through your spirit. To receive that goodness you possess. To be that child of God that you want me to be Lord.

Rise to the glory of the Lord.

1 Thessalonians: 4

When the last trump has been sounded. We shall be forever with the Lord. he is the first and the last, the beginning and the end. He is also the alpha and the Omega. The eternal God he is the lover of mankind. When we look at the Lord this way. We see him for who he really is. When I Look at him this way I see him for who he really is. I Think about what he did on that old rugged cross. How he loves all of mankind. He told the thief on his right hand. The Bible Tells us in Luke 23:43. Verily I say unto thee. Today shalt thou be with me in paradise.

Prayer

Father help me to stay focused on you. To share my faith with others that do not know you.

Jesus the true Messiah

1 John 5: 1-13
Key verse: Luke 2: 11

Jesus is the true living Messiah. Luke 2 shows us how the Father sent his Son into the world. He came as an infant. He is still the Son of God. He is the true and perfect sacrifice. He came for all of mankind. In 1 John 5:7 shows us how he is the Son of God. In John 14:6 the Bible tells us that he is the way the truth and the life. When we look at him as the true Messiah. We should be sharing our faith with others. In Titus 3:4-7. In verse four the Bible tells us. But after that the kindness and love of God our Savior toward man appeared. We need to ask ourselves what that Passage tells us. We also need to share Titus 3: 4-7 with others that do not know the Lord Jesus. Tell them that he is the true Messiah.

Prayer

Lord help me to not focus on the sin. That hampers my relationship with Christ Jesus. Lord, I pray for the lost and dying world that we live in.

The manifested Grace of God and spiritual gifts of the Holy Ghost.

Romans 12:1-8
`1 Corithians 12: 1-10
Key verse Romans 12:3

We need to be teachable in our spirit. Then the lord can show us our spiritual gifts that we are to receive. We need to yield to the Holy Ghost. When we do, we know when to obtain the gifts of the Spirit. We obtain our gifts through the Holy Ghost. By engaging in prayer and also looking in the scripture. Then we receive the understanding of the gifts. In Romans 12: 1-8 tells us about some of the gifts. We receive our gifts through our faith in our Lord. I received my gift of preaching and teaching. I stepped out in faith when I acted on the preaching and teaching. The Lord will honor our faith in this area. I am challenging you on your faith to step out and receive what the Lord has intended for you to receive.

Prayer

Lord help me not to focus on the sin that hinders me from receiving.

Who is the Comforter?

John 14: 16-31
Key verse: 1 John 5:7 KJV.

Who is this Comforter? He is the third person of the trinity. He is the Holy Ghost, the Spirit of the living God. When we accept Christ as your Lord and Savior. He teaches us the Holy Word of the one true God. Jesus promised us the receiving of the Holy Ghost. When he ascended to the Father. In Acts 1: 1-10 we see that promise received.

Prayer

Lord help me to call on you through the Holy Ghost.

Do we live in a Lions Den

Daniel 6: 1-28
Key Verse: Romans 12:12

Are we men and women of prayer ? We need to ask ourselves that question. I know my life goes better if I bathe it with prayer. When we pray we are having a conversation with the God of the universe. He loves us so much he longs to have that intimate relationship with us. In Mark 11:24 the Bible tells us that we need to forgive others. So our Father in heaven may forgive our sin. When we approach the throne of grace we need to have a clean heart. So prayers are heard and answered. We also need to be in his will. We need to remember what he did for Daniel. Because of his faith and love for God. As long as we are in his will he will answer our prayers. When we go to pray we need to have faith and love for God.

Prayer

When we go to pray we need to have the faith and love for God that Daniel had.

Make away for the Lord

Isaiah 40: 1-13
Key verse: John 1: 1

There was a man and his name was John. John the Baptist is his name. He was dressed in camel's hair and feasted on locusts and wild honey. He was a humble man. He was sent to prepare the way of the Lord. In Luke 3: He said behold there is the Lamb of God which taketh away the sin of the world. He says I Baptize with water. He will baptize with the Holy Ghost and fire from heaven. That is why we should speak of Jesus. He is the true God and savior Jesus Christ. The Bible tells us in Titus 3: 5. Not by works of righteousness which we have done. But by the washing of regeneration and the renewing of the Holy Ghost. That is why we need to witness a lost and dying world. We need to share John 3:16 with them.

Prayer

Lord help me to be that witness that you want me to be.

The Tongue of love and Grace verses the razor tongue.

Psalms 52: 1-9
Key verse: James 3:8

As Christians we are to speak thanksgiving and praise. We are to think before we speak. The Bible tells us in James 1: 19 wherefore my beloved brethren. Let every man be swift to hear, slow to speak and slow to wrath. When we focus on this teaching from God's word. We can be a true witness for Jesus.The Lord has shown me how it is so important to think before I speak. If we do say something that we are not supposed to say we should ask for forgiveness and make it right with the parties involved. When we do it we have peace about the situation. Also our witness is maintained.

Prayer

Father help me to listen to others. Make sure we think before we speak.

The Shelter of the Most High

Psalms 91: 1-16
Key Verse: Psalms 23:4

As we go through our lives.We have a mighty loving and caring God. When I feel down. I remember what the Lord tells me in Psalms 91:4. When I seek his peace and love. I feel like I can defeat whatever the world has to offer. Then I am set to do the Lords service. I Look at what the Lord has for me to do. As I walk through the valley of the shadow of death. I will fear evil. Thy rod and thy staff comfort me. That is found in Psalms 23: 4-5. When we are under his wing as it says in Psalms 91. Also in Philippians 4:13: I can do all things through Christ which strengtheneth me.

Prayer

Lord, I pray that you give me the strength I need. Then I ask thee that I may be under your wing.

Let your Light so Shine before Men.

Matthew 5: 13-16 / Key verse Matthew 5: 16

When I think about how important it is to let my light shine before men. So you can see the glory that is given to your dear Lord. When we let our light shine. We can bring glory and honor and praise to the Lord our God. Then we can be a true witness of the Lord Jesus. So then we are able to reach the lost and dying world. Then the lost can find the salvation of the Lord. That is why our witness is so important. It is also important to share John 3:16. When we show them the love of Jesus. People can receive what they are looking for in their life. Then we are truly serving the Lord we love.

Prayer

Lord, I ask that your light will shine right through me. Then others may see me as your servant and your child.

That old Rugged Cross

Luke 23: 1-56
Key verse: Luke 23: 43-46
Isaiah 53: 4-6

What does the cross mean to me? It means I have a new life. I really want everyone to recieve Jesus as their Lord and Savior. Our responsibility is to be a good witness. We cannot fathom what our Lord went through. We only know what the Bible tells us. When we look at that passage in Isaiah 53 verse 6. All we like sheep have gone astray; we have turned everyone to his own way; and the lord has laid on him the iniquity of us all. When we look at this passage we can kinda understand what he went through. When we choose to sin. We are crucifying the Lord all over again. We need to think about our actions before we engage. We should have a heart of repentance.

Prayer

Lord help me to be that good witness for you.

Who is the Rock

Psalms: 92: 1-15
Key verse: Psalms 92:2,15

I look at that rock that rock I see is Christ Jesus. As it states in the Bible in verse 15. It shows that the Lord is upright. There is no unrighteousness through the blood of the lamb and the word of his testimony. We look at the Lord Jesus as the perfect sacrifice. Because he is the perfect sacrifice. In Psalms 40:2 he brought me up also out of a horrible pit, out of the miry clay, and set my feet upon a rock,and established my goings.When I look at that Rock of my salvation. When I was a boy. I Learned who my Savior was. As I look to Christ Jesus and see who he really is. It makes me want to share my faith with others. We have been commissioned by the Lord Jesus because of his sacrifice on the cross. We all need to look at our faith and share the plan of salvation.

Prayer

Lord help me to share my faith and turn to you.

The Eye Of The Storm

Matthew 14:22-33; Mark 6:45-52; John 6:1-14.

When we feel down or depressed in life. We do not look to Jesus for comfort. We usually go to outside sources. Such as a close friend or secular council. We should be seeking Godly counsel. When we are looking unto Jesus the Author and finisher of our faith; who for the joy that was set before him endured the cross despising the shame, and is set down at the right hand of the throne of God; Hebrews 12:2. When Peter took his eyes off Jesus. He began to sink into the sea of Galilee. If Peter would have stayed focused on Jesus. He would not have started sinking into the sea. Sometimes that is what we do. That's why the word of God is so important. Prayer is also very important. We should not want Jesus to be our last resort.

Prayer

Father help me to stay focused on you Lord. Thank you for always being there for me.

The Wisdom of God

1 Kings 3: 16-28

How often in our life. Do we try to figure out things on our own? All we have to do is call on Gods' wisdom. When we look at King Solomon's decision. He knew the real love of the true mother. She was willing to give her son to the other Harlot. To save the baby's life. King Soloman saw her wisdom and love for her child. He was using the divine wisdom that the Lord blessed him with. In James 3:13 the Bible shows us. In James 3:13 the Bible tells us. Who is a wise man and endowed with knowledge among you? Let him shew out of a good conversation his works with meekness of wisdom. When we look at that passage. We see how important meekness is and Gods' wisdom is. We need to look at the proverbs. The Lord really shows us his wisdom in the proverbs. That gives us an opportunity to share his wisdom with others. We can also use his wisdom in our lives.

Prayer

Father help me to cling to your wisdom.

The Faith of a Mustard Seed

Hebrews 11: 1-3

Gracious Lord, I Thank you for your word. Psalms 119:97 comes to mind. As we meditate on God's word. That increases our faith in our precious Lord. The parable of the Mustard seed comes to mind. Matthew 13: 31-32 speaks about the parable how the seed was sown in the field and grew into a large tree and the birds were nesting in the tree. Which means our faith can grow like a tree. The Lord is the one that makes our faith grow. The mustard seed is the least of all seeds. The more we exercise our faith the more it grows. We learn to trust and believe in the Lord Jesus. I challenge you to exercise your faith in the Lord Jesus.

Prayer

Father I ask you to increase my faith

The faith of Moses Aaron and Hur and Joshua
Exodus 17: 8-16 yyy
Father helped me to have the faith that these men did.
In Exodus 17:11-12 and it came to pass when Moses held up his hands -

A Devotional Throughout the day

The confession of sin

Text Psalms 32

When we confess our sin unto the Lord. We are being true obedient children of God. In 1 John 1:9. The Bible tells us that if we confess our sin he is faithful and just to forgive our sins he is faithful and just to cleanse us from all unrighteousness. We need to remember; what Jesus did for us on the cross of calvary. Because if we don't confess our sins. How can we say we are the child of the living God. We know the Holy Ghost will convict us of our sin. When we have that forgiving heart our Messiah can use us to lead others to CHRIST.

Prayer

Father help me to have a forgiving heart.

A Christmas to remember

Text: Luke 2: 1-21 Key verse
Matthew 3:3

Some 2,000 years here or there was the greatest gift given to mankind. It was the birth of the Lord Jesus Christ. When I was a kid I read out of the Gospel of Luke. About the birth of our Savior. In Isaiah 9:6 was the prophecy of the birth of our Lord. For unto us a son is given and the government shall be upon his shoulder and his name shall be called wonderful counselor the mighty God, the everlasting father, the prince of peace. This is the time of the year we need to share our faith. We also need to be there for the less fortunate. This is the most incredible love. All of mankind will ever see or hear. Let us be people of prayer. For the lost and dying world.

Prayer

Father helps me to remember Jesus through the season. Father helped me to want to pray and witness the lost and dying world. I love you deeply my Lord.

Am I In the bosom of Abraham

Text: Romans 4: 1-25 Key verse: Genesis 12: 1-4

Are we exercising our faith as Abraham did in Genesis 12: 1-4. We see the Lord for who he really is. I always think about when Abraham was going to offer Issac as the sacrifice. Abraham showed the Lord how much he believed and loved the God of the universe. He also waited for his son to pass the birth right onto Isaac. So the many nations could be carried on because of the faith that both of them had. The Lord provided the sacrifice. The Bible showed us in Genesis 22. That he had a ram tangled in the thicket. The Lord stopped Abraham from thrusting the dagger into Issac's chest. My first wife and I exercised our faith that we had a 11,000.00 medical bill that the insurance company would not cover. We prayed and our prayers were answered. What a mighty God we serve.That is why we should always be strengthening our relationship with our Lord.

Prayer

Thank you lord for dying for me and being there for me.

The Good Shepherd

Matthew 9:34-38 Key Verse John 10:10-15
Psalms 23:1-6

The Lord tells us in his Word. That he is the Good Shepherd of the sheep. Our shepherd has compassion on us. By which we don't deserve. In psalms 23 King David wrote about the staff. The staff is His loving grace and peace. Because without that peace we have nothing but turmoil and unrest in our lives. As you see in the text, how Jesus is there to help and direct them. I Know in my life I asked him for help in my financial situation. With a 11,000.00 hospital bill and the Lord seen to it that the bill was paid in full. We should be excited about sharing our faith. Also we should give glory to the Lord in every situation.

Prayer

Father help me to remember your Son that he is the Good Shepherd.

The Burning Bush

Text: Exodus 3
1 Peter 1:15-16

In My Life I always tried to do things my own way. The lord showed me I need to count on him. Because he is a Holy God. When you count on him. Your life can be a Holy life;because when you look at God's word you can see how the Lord wants us to live. When we look at Exodus 3. We see how Moses was drawn to the burning bush. Because of the holiness of the Lord. He had a mission for Moses to deliver the Hebrews from Egypt. Moses felt inadequate but the Lord knew that he could accomplish the mission. Because he trusted God to speak through his brother Arraon. We need to learn from Moses' mistakes. We need to follow through with what the Lord has for us.

Prayer

Lord help me to trust in you. To live a holy life. Also to look at you for who you really are.

The Mercy of God

Text: Psalms: 103

When I look to the mercy of God. I see God in a different way. I know I would be going to Hell. If I Hadn't turned to the Lord Jesus. In the Gospel of Luke in the twenty third chapter in the 43 verse.Jesus tells the theif on the right. Verily I say unto thee, today shalt thou be with me in paradise. When we look at what Jesus has done for us all. We see nothing but unconditional love and mercy. Also we see his mercy and faithfulness of our Lord and God. In Lamentations 3:23. The Bible tells us that he is new every morning. Great is his faithfulness. We should look at Psalms 145: 8-9. How he is gracious and compassionate and full of mercy . He is also good to all and his tender mercies are over all his works. That is why we can rely on him.

Prayer

Lord help me to remember and rely on your love and mercy and faithfulness.

Love One Another

Text: 1 John 3: 11-24
Key Verse: 1 John 3:16

The Lord Jesus wants all to love one another. We should be praying for one another and building up one another. The Lord's word tells us in Romans 13 distributing to the necessity of the saints, given to hospitality. When we are there to meet the needs of others. We are in the will of God. Because that is what Jesus would do. That also strengthens our faith. Also strenghtens the person or persons we are helping. Also in Gods' word we see in James 1:27. The Bible states that pure religion and undefiled before God and the Father is this. To visit the fatherless and the widows in their affliction and to keep himself unspotted from the world.

Prayer

Father help me love others. Father, sometimes it is hard to love the unlovable.

The Importance Of Prayer

Text: James 5:13-20
Key verse: Mark 11: 22-26

As we take a look at our prayer life. We can really see how strong our relationship with our God and King is. Because if we take a look at Daniel. In Daniel 6 we see how much he loved our God and King. When they told him to refrain from praying to the Lord. He chose not to listen to King Darius and the officals of Babylon. So they decided to throw him in the lion's den. The Lord sent an angel to Daniel to save him from the lions. Our faith and obedience should be that of Daniels. I know when I approach the throne of grace. I long for his presence. My relationship will get stronger.

Prayer

Lord help me to have a stronger prayer life.

The Second Coming of Christ

Text: Revalation 19
Key Verse: Jude15
2 Thessalonian: 3: 1-5

The second coming why is it so important? That we reflect on our Lord and Savior Jesus Christ. My relationship with Jesus counts on not only the death, resurrection and ascension are important in my walk with Jesus. His second coming is also important. Because he will be coming at the sound of the trumpet. The Bible Says in Thessalonians 4: 15 -18. That we need to share our faith. But not to stop there we should tell them about the second coming of Christ. That is really important that everyone knows that we come in contact with. I Want to close with this thought. That we have been commissioned to make disciples of all nations as the Bible declares. Also encourage others to witness about our Lord and Savior Jesus Christ. Like it says in Titus 3:3-7.

Prayer

Heavenly Father helps me to share Jesus with others.

Jesus at the Right hand of God

Text: Acts 1: 9-11
Key Verse: Acts 7: 55-56

When we think of Jesus we know the Holy Bible tells us that we have the promise of eternal life. Eternal life is there for the taking. All we have to do is believe and confess our sins that Jesus died on the cross for our sins. He also rose on the third day according to the scriptures. We should be there to share our faith with others. Because we don't know who knows Jesus. Not only friends and family. We need to be led by the Holy Spirit. We need to make sure it's the right time to share our faith. Because everyone needs to know the Savior. 1 John 5:11 the Bible tells us. And this is the record that God hath given to us eternal life, and this life is in his Son.

Prayer

Lord Help Me To be that sound witness. For my blessed Jesus

Jesus the Author and Finisher of our faith

Text: Hebrews 12:1-4
Key Verse: Hebrews 11:6

What is faith we need to ask ourselves that question.Why is it important that Jesus is our auther. What does the author write? He writes his love on our hearts. He also writes words of instruction and encouragement. That is the foundation of the love we have for him. Why is it so important that we see what he is really doing for us? That Jesus is truly the author of my life. I Try to know the truth and power of his words. Prayer also plays a big part in my walk with the Lord. I want to leave you with this thought. We need to believe and love and trust in our beloved Lord Jesus Christ.

Prayer

Lord help me increase my faith in you because of you.

King of Kings and Lord of Lords'

Text: Revelation 19: 11-18
Key Verse: Revelation 19: 16

There have been mighty men of valor. Such as KIng David and King Solomen. Henry the Eighth and Louie the 14th. To name a few but they are mere men. They have passed on to the other side. There is one king that is eternal. That is King Jesus. The Bible says he wears many crowns. He is the King of Kings and the Lord of Lords. In Revelation 19:12 he is going to come back for his church. There is still time to join him as one of his children. All you have to do is look into the Bible at Romans 10: 8-13. If you believe that Jesus died on the cross for your sins. In Romans 10:13 the Bible tells us. For whosoever calls on the name of the Lord shall be saved.

Prayer

Lord help me to remember your Son Jesus. Is my Savior and Lord. Help me to pray for the lost.

Why is Prayer a Gift

Text: Jeremiah 33: 1-3
Key Verse: 1 Timothy 2: 5
Mark 11: 24-26

When I look to my Lord for guidance expecially with the virus in our midst. We need Jesus all the more. We should turn to him in prayer. When we approach the throne of grace. With our needs and requests. We know our God is there to hear our request's. We need to ask for forgiveness of our sins. So he will hear our prayers. Prayer is a gift through the salvation from our sins. Through the death and resurrection of the Lord Jesus Christ. The Jesus of the Bible. When we pray we need to end our prayer in Jesus' name. Because we cannot come to the Fathers presence except in the name of Jesus. Because he died for our sins. Because the Father cannot look at our sin. That is why he sent Jesus to die in our place.

Prayer

Father, I thank you for the gift of prayer. Through the name of Jesus. By his death and resurrection.

The Fabulous Morning

Text: John 20: 11-19
Key Verse: J0hn 20: 19

What a fabulous morning. The resurrection of our Lord and Savior Jesus Christ. In John 20: 11-19. When Mary came to the tomb and saw the two angels where have they laid my Lord. She turned and saw the Lord Standing there. The Lord asked her why are you weeping. Then he asked her who she was seeking. She said I am seeking my Lord. So I can take him away. Then the Lord said Mary. Then she said Rabboni. Which is to say Master. Then he told her not to touch him; he had not gone to the Father. He said I Ascend unto my Father and your Father; and to my God and your God. Then he appeared to his disciples and said peace be with you. That is the true story about our Lord and Savior Jesus Christ.

Prayer

Father helps me to share my faith with others. Help Me to tell them about the resurrection story.

The Love and Friendship of God

Text: John 15: 9-14
Key Verse: John 15: 13

When I Look to God. I see him as my Savior and God and Friend. With the world in utter chaos we have a true friend in our God and savior Jesus Christ. He has been there for me and my family. The world needs to cling to the Lord Jesus. He is a true friend and Savior of the world. He is the way the truth and the life. When we focus on our friend God and Savior. We know we need to repent of our sins so we can accept the Lord Jesus as our Lord and Savior. Because he chose us we did not choose him. In Romans 10: 8-13. Paul tells us how important it is to accept Jesus as Lord. Then He will be our Savior Lord, and Friend. For all of eternity. Because we will be spending eternity somewhere. Either it will be in heaven or hell. We Need to choose Jesus to go to heaven.

Prayer

Father I pray that I choose Jesus as Lord and friend, and Savior. So that my eternity is set.

Kevin Bandoli

The God Of The Mountain Top

Text: Exodus 3: 1-22
Key Verse: Exodus 3: 5

Who is that God of the mountain top? How are we to find out who this God is? This is the God of all creation. As we see in the book of Genesis. We look around us and see the Lord at work. The purity of the new falling snow, the turning of the leaves on the trees; and falling rain and the dew on the ground. We see the love and grace of our Lord. He spoke to Moses in verse five that he was entering into Holy ground. He has that majesty that we don't completely understand. He does not only meet our spiritual needs but also our physical needs.When we look at Matthew 6: 25-34. He shows us how are physical needs are met. In John 3: 1-18. How are spiritual needs are met.

Prayer

Lord, I am thankful and grateful for what you have done for me.

A Devotional Throughout the day

He Supplies all our Needs

Text: Matthew 6: 25-34

When we feel in despair because we are lacking in our physical needs. Jesus wants us to call on him. So we should not feel like we are unable for our needs to be met. Because Jesus is Jehovah Jirea our provider. When we call on him in prayer, needs will be met. Not always the way we think. He always comes through with what we need. My first wife and I were struggling finacially. The church we were attending had a meeting and gave us the funds we needed. My wife and I were so surprised and blessed. At the christian love that was shown to us. You never know how the Lord can impact your life. I Want to close with. That we should love our neighbor as our self Matthew 22:39.

Prayer

Father help me to love and trust you. To always think of one another.

Lead Me to the Rock

Text: Psalms 61

When I read Psalms 61. I see how my Lord is my King and Rock. There was a time in my life when I just went through the motions. I Didn't realize that he was my Rock and Savior. Accepted him as Lord and Savior of my life. In the book of Titus in the third chapter and in verse 4 and 5. The Bible tells us that we are to accept him as Lord and Savior. By exercising our faith in Him that he died for our sins on that old rugged cross. Then he rose again on the third day for the remission of our sins. Then he ascended to heaven and is standing at the right hand of the Father. He had to go to the father with his blood as a sacrifice for our sins. I want to close with this point. That is why he is my Rock and Savior. Also he can be your Rock and Savior.

Prayer

Father I pray that I can witness to others how you are my Rock and Savior.

A Devotional Throughout the day

The Passion of the Lord our God

Text: Matthew 22: 36-40
Key Verse: Titus 3: 4-7

When we look at our life does it reflect the salvation messege. When we go to work or school or are retired we should reflect the Savior's love. Because when we accept Jesus we are filled with his Holy Spirit. We are to live our life through the Holy Spirit. We have to remember that we have a sin nature. So we are prone to sin. That is why we need to be led by the Spirit. That is why we need to follow the Holy Bible. That is how we reflect the salvation message. In John 9: 35-41 the Lord showed the Pharisees that they were spiritually blinded by traditions of men. They were not following the teachings of Jesus. So we need to be good witnesses for the Lord Jesus.

Prayer

Lord help me to reflect the love and admiration for you and my fellow man.

The Love and Forgiveness of Others in these Peerless Times'

Text: Matthew 18: 25-35
Key Verse: Matthew 18: 27

When we look at this world and see all the rioting and shootings. We need to look at what the Bible says all about the violence and unrest in this world. That our Lord died for everyone in this world. Even for the ones' that have rejected him. Because there is still a chance for them to repent and turn from their sin. So we should have a forgiving heart. Even if we have been hurt very deeply. The Lord has forgiven us of our sins. When we have a forgiving heart; that is what the Lord wants us to do. When we have that forgiving heart. The world will see our love and compassion that we have for them. The Lord will be pleased with what we have done for him and others. We need to witness Jesus and show them the love of God

Prayer

Lord help me to love and forgive others and to be the witness he wants us to be.

The God of Peace

Text : John 14: 27
Key Verse: John 16: 33

May the God of peace be with you always. When I feel down I know I Can Count on the Lord Jesus to give me the peace I am seeking. When the lord Jesus entered my life I knew there was more to life than what I was experiencing. My life was full of utter chaos. I turned to the things of the world hoping I would find what I Was looking for. Then I met a christian brother. He had what I Was looking for. I Asked him how I could obtain it. He told me I had to start seeking out Jesus. I Asked him how to do that. He said I needed to seek Jesus through prayer and the reading of the Bible. Also through gospel and christian music. I started to seek him out. I started to see John 14:27 and John 16:33 come to life in my life. All of us can have that heavenly peace through the Lord Jesus Christ. I Challenge you to seek that peace in your life.

Prayer

Father I pray that whoever reads this devotional finds this peace that you freely give. I pray they freely receive it.

The Way the Truth the Life

Text: John 14: 1-6
Key Verse: John 14: 6

I Was living in Eau Claire WI. It was Easter time in 1969. I was at a Baptist Church. When I was 8 years old I was at an Easter egg hunt at the church. The Pastor asked me if I knew who Jesus was. If he was my Lord and Savior of my life. I Told him I Was not sure about my relationship with the Lord Jesus. Then he took me into his office to explain the message of salvation to me. Then he asked me if I Wanted to ask Jesus into my heart. I Was not sure if I Wanted to accept Jesus as Lord. So he opened up the Gospel to me by reading passages that pertained to salvation. After thinking about what I Had heard. I finally decided to pray and accept Jesus as my Savior and Lord. Then when I Got home I Shared my new found faith and salvation. I told mom that I Was going to be a Pastor someday. The reason I shared my life changing story. We all have a responsibility to share the Gospel with others.

Prayer

Father help me to be bold and share my faith with others.

Selfishness and Hostile Anger is not of God

Text: James 1: 19-20
Key Verse: Proverbs 15:1

When I look at others I see they are created by God. Whether they are acting with a positive or negative attitude. I love them anyway. Because when you approach them with a smile you can change hostile situations. We need to look at the situation as Jesus would. How do we know we are looking at the situation the way our Lord would look at it. We need to look at the word of God. When we do that we are showing them the love of Christ. We will be a good witness for Christ. Others will want to have what we have. Because it is a good witness to share with others also. That is what Zacheus shows us in Luke 7: 1-11. In Matthew 5:16 the Bible tells us that we are to let our light so shine before men, that they may see your good works, and glorify your Father which is in heaven.

Prayer

Father help me to treat others as you would

Loving God or Loving the Lusts of Man

Text: 1 John 4: 7-21
Key Verse: 1 John 4:10

What is the love of God? When we see what he did on the cross for us. That truly is the love of God. In John 11 when Jesus came to see that Lazarus had died he wept. That is an example of the love of God. They told Jesus that Lazarus had died four days prior. Jesus told them to roll the stone away. Then he told Lazarus to come out and he did. The lusts of men are to fill their evil desires. There was a time in my life when I put conditions on my love for others. I had an attitude that it was my way or you could go down the highway. We should change those things in our life that draws us away from God. We should pray for others that are looking at themselves only.

Prayer

Lord help me to keep focused on your love.

The Naughtiness of Man verses the Goodness of God

Text: James 1:19-27
Key Verse: James 1:21

What is the Naughtiness of man? Some might call it sin. Some might call it a good time. According to the Bible it is sin. Because when we sin we are separated from God. He still loves us in spite of our sin. When we follow his word he is pleased with us. Then we can be a good witness for him. When we obey his word others see that if they are having a rough day. They can see how a child of God lives. They can have an impact on others also. So the better road to go down is to follow the goodness of God. In James 1: 22 we are to be doers of the word and not hearers only. The Lord loves you so much he wants the best for you. I will close with this: we are to love God and love others.

Prayer

Father help me to follow the goodness and love of God.

The God of the Bible verses the god of the World

Text: John 8: 42-59
Key Verse: Isaiah 14: 12-14

Who is the God of the Bible? He is the creator of the world. He is the Savior of the world. He is the lion of Judah. He is the root of Jesse. He is a loving God and the God of Heaven. God sent his Son as an atoning sacrifice for our sins. Because our sin is what separates us from the Father because God the Father is so Holy he can not look on sin. He wants all of us to spend eternity with him. All you have to do is accept Jesus as Lord. The way you do that is to ask forgiveness of your sins. Because Jesus paid the price of our sins on the cross. In Roman 10: 8-13 shows us how much we need Jesus to have eternal life. The god of the world is the devil. He wants to take us to hell along with him. Hell is real in Revelation 20 John shows us that hell is real. I hope you make the right choice between heaven and hell.

Prayer

Father, I am asking for forgiveness of my sin. I am standing in faith that you died for my sins Jesus.

The Way To Repentance

Text: Isaiah 53: 4-9
Key Verse: Isaiah: 53: 6

Have you ever asked where you were going when you died? When I was a boy I started reading the Christmas story out of Luke 2. There were many things I Didn't understand about the Lord. My mom and grandparents had me going to church. I knew in my heart there was more to this person they called Jesus. It was the spring of 1969 I went to this Baptist Church in Eau Claire WI. Out of all the kids there the Pastor keyed on me. He asked me if I knew Jesus as my Lord and Savior. I told him I was not sure. He shared out of the Bible. I was certain I Wanted to know Jesus as my Lord and Savior. So we prayed and I received Jesus as Lord and Savior. The reason it is so important that we receive Jesus as Lord our eternity depends on it. If we don't accept him as Savior we are going to hell we have to do this before we die.

Prayer

Father I accept your Son Jesus as my Savior Lord.

The Faith of the Centurion

Text: Luke 7: 1-10
Key Verse: Luke 7: 9

What is our faith? Why do we believe the way we do? Because our faith is so important in our walk with Christ. That is the vehicle that drives us to Christ. Because when we walk in that valley that Psalms 23 talks about we sometimes feel alone. Our life should not be driven by our feelings. It should be driven by our faith. Because the faith the centurion had is an example to us that we need to follow. We should be in total submission to the leading of the Holy Spirit in our life. We can never be led astray. Our faith is increased when we pray and read the Bible and worship him in gospel and Christian music. I want to leave you with this thought. In Romans 10: 17. Faith comes by hearing and hearing by the Word of God.

Prayer

Father help me to exercise my faith.

God's Love Toward His People

Text: John 13: 4-11
Key Verse: John 13: 34-35

What is the love of God toward his people? In Exodus chapters 13 and 14 the Bible tells us that He led the Isrealites through the desert by a pillar of fire. He also saved Daniel from the lion's den. Those are a couple of examples of God's love. When we look at the mercy of God he didn't have to save us from hell. That is his unconditional love for all of us. He loves us so much that he sent his only begotten Son into the world to die for our sins.We see the example when Jesus washed the disciples feet. In our text we see he even loved his betrayer. In Luke 6: 27-28 we are to love and pray for them. Joseph in the book of Genesis how he loved his brothers even though they wanted to kill him. Instead they sold him into slavery.

Prayer

Father help me to love you more deeply. Also love others.

The Crucifixion Of Our Lord

Text: John 19: 1-42
Key Verse: John 19 : 36-37

Who is this Jesus of Nazareth? As we meditate on him. What does the Bible tell us about this Jesus. The Bible tells us that he came to die on the cross for all of mankind. He is the King of the Jews and the King of Kings and the Lord of Lords. He loved us so much that he died for you personally. The Bible tells us that he is the perfect sacrifice for our sins. Because he was sinless. He is the Lamb of God that takes away the sin of the world. He was chosen by the Father God. We should give him all the glory that is due him. I want to leave you with this thought. He has given us eternity with the Father God.

Prayer

Father, thank you for sending your Son to die for us.
Jesus I Thank you for dying for me.

The Holiness Of God

Text: 1 Peter 1: 15-17
Psalms 96: 1-13
Key Verse: Psalms 96:9

What is the Holiness of God? We need to ask ourselves about the Holiness of God. When we look at the holiness of God. We in know way line up to him know man can measure up to our God. The only way we can see our Holy God is that we have to accept Jesus as Lord and Savior. Because of our sin we cannot approach the throne of grace. We cannot pray to Him unless we pray in Jesus name. Because Jesus is the sinless Lamb of God. Which takes away the sin of the world. We need to proclaim the holiness of God. We also need to witness about our holy God. We should worship our God and read his word and pray to him. We should find a time of day that is our quiet time with our Holy God.

Prayer

Father help me to find time to spend with you daily. Also share my faith with others.

From the Author

Kevin M Bandoli

I hope you were blessed by this Devotional.

    I am blessed that you took the time to check out . What the Lord has Inspired me to write for you to bless you. I hope you will tell others about this Devotional.

Milton Keynes UK
Ingram Content Group UK Ltd.
UKHW030748121124
451094UK00013B/881